The Silent Storm:

Finding Faith in the

Chaos of Grief

Sara Hopson

ISBN: 978-0-578-68738-4

Contents of this book are works of nonfiction. Some names have been changed to preserve privacy.

Cover image by Kayla Hlavin
Book design by Sara Hopson

Printed by DiggyPOD, Inc., in the United States of America.

First printing edition 2020.

www.faithingrief.com

Acknowledgements

First, a thank you to all the people that made this book possible. From family and friends who encouraged me to write it in the first place to all those involved in taking my words and making them a physical thing. I want to specifically thank John Da Via, Mark Brown and John Opalewski for their time and effort in editing, Kayla Hlavin for the beautiful cover art, and all the hearts willing to be vulnerable enough to give me different perspectives.

Second, I want to thank you: my reader. While I hate that you even have to read a book like mine, I appreciate that you have put some trust in me to help ease your pain in this confusing time. Thank you for allowing me to speak into your grief.

Contents

Introduction

Before I say anything else, I want to say I am so sorry. There are no words to adequately explain your loss. No matter whom you have lost, it is significant. If you are able, please find someone to talk to. Find a counselor, therapist, or support group in your area. As Henry Wadsworth Longfellow said, "There is no grief like the grief that does not speak."[1]

The experience from which I write is the sudden unexpected loss of my husband Travis. You will read more of my story throughout the book. While your loss may have been a spouse, a child, a parent, a friend, or someone else, I pray this book may be of some help and comfort to you.

I have written this book to suit your needs as much as possible. Each chapter ends with reflection questions. These are intended to help you examine your own grief and give you an idea of where to go from here. The chapters are also shorter. In my grief, I did not have the concentration to focus for more than a few minutes. I tried to be as concise as possible to give you the best insight I can. Between chapters, you will find interviews from others who have lost loved ones. Some have lost children, others have lost parents. Some are like me and have lost a spouse. My hope is between my commentary and theirs, you will find comfort and peace.

Anything written in this book is from my own experience, or that of those I interviewed. No content should be taken as professional counseling.

My story

To fully understand my situation and how I learned what I did, I have to give you some background. This is my story.

I was the girl who never thought she would marry. I enjoyed living my life and doing my own thing. When my dad, by chance, found out a childhood friend of mine was attending a church close to where I was living for college, I didn't go to find him with the hopes of finding the man of my dreams. I didn't even have a made-up ideal picture of a man. When my dad told me Travis was going to a church nearby, my thought was simply, "Okay, I haven't seen this kid in thirteen years, but why not?" I remembered going to Sunday school with Travis when we were little, but I hadn't seen or spoken to him since we were seven years old. For old times' sake, I went to that church on a Sunday morning. I hated it. Honestly, I just wanted to get out of there. I remember leaving thinking, "What was I doing? I don't even know what he looks like now." I decided to give it one more chance, so I went back the next Sunday. Thanks to Facebook, I recognized his brother. Travis' family was there, but he was at work. Reluctantly, I decided to return that evening. When I did, Travis was waiting for me. We sat through service, although I will admit it was difficult to wait to talk to him. After service, we went out for ice cream. Our first official date was four days later.

Fast-forward a few years, and what I thought would never be was about to happen. In June 2015, I became Travis' wife. We were able to buy a cute little tri-level house and make it into our home. Not long after, we added our fur baby, an adorable terrier-mix puppy we named Buddy. He was, always will be, our first baby. I never wanted kids, so Buddy was it for me. Travis, on the other hand, wanted nothing more than to be a dad. It took him a couple of years, but he changed my mind. No one else on this planet could have convinced me to have a child, but Travis did. In 2017, I got pregnant. It was a very difficult pregnancy with many complications, including pre-eclampsia. Travis went to every appointment with me, not because I asked him to, but because he wanted to. We moved into a new house, and just two weeks later, our son Cole was born early. He stayed in NICU for a little bit, but he is healthy. Travis was overjoyed to have a son.

I have no way to adequately describe the type of dad Travis was. He poured more love into our boy than many dads do over an entire lifetime. We often spoke of the plans we had together. We were going to go to Hawaii for our tenth anniversary. Travis was going to teach our son how to build and fix car engines. We were going to grow old together and enjoy grandkids. Was our marriage perfect? No. Did we argue? Sometimes. But we always loved each other and worked to ensure our marriage was strong. I can honestly say (and many others have said) that Travis and I had a marriage that many people only hope for. Little did we know how soon our life together would come to an end.

November 26, 2018. It was a normal day. I got up with Cole in the morning like I always did; I usually let Travis sleep in a little. Cole and I woke him up around 10 AM. We had a few hours to enjoy together before I went back to bed. That was the last time I saw Travis. He kept Cole so I could sleep for my midnight shift that night. Travis took Cole to his mom's house when he went to work that afternoon. Nothing was unusual; nothing was out of place. I spoke to Travis on my way to work, and that was the last time I heard his voice. As always, my mother-in-law brought Cole back home to put him to bed. Travis got home from work, checked on Cole in his crib, said goodbye to his mom, and went to bed. Still, no one knew anything was wrong. When I got home in the morning, Buddy was whining. He was in our bedroom as always, but he would not typically whine when I got home. I remember walking by the door, saying, "It's alright, Bud, it's just me." I walked into the room, and Buddy was not at the door waiting for me, which was also unusual. At this point, I had that sinking feeling something was very wrong. I turned on the light and at first didn't even see Travis. Buddy was sitting at the corner of the bed, looking between the floor and me. I looked down to find Travis facedown on the ground. My brain instantly switched from wife to nurse. I put Buddy in his crate, unlocked the front door, and called 911. I ran back into our room and turned Travis over.

One look and I knew. Travis had a long history of seizures, and one seizure took him away from me. I knew he was gone, and I knew it had been hours. I had my phone on speaker talking to the dispatcher. I started compressions, but I knew they were futile. Nothing was going to save my husband. Paramedics arrived just six minutes after I made the call. The rest of the morning was a blur of questions and uniforms: police officers, detectives, and medical examiners. My entire life had been shattered in a matter of moments. Every expectation for my life was gone. My husband, just 29 years old, was gone. All the dreams and plans we had together were stripped away. My life went from really great to a nightmare with no warning. And all I could think was why?

But Why?

That's the first thing we ask, isn't it? Once the reality of death sets in, we instantly want to know why. Why did he/she have to die? Why did this have to happen to us? I think the question of why is completely expected and normal. We want some explanation for this pain as if an explanation might somehow make it easier to accept. Travis was only 29 years old. He was supposed to have decades ahead of him. So why did his life have to be cut short? This is often asked when the person who passed was young, especially if the person was a child. While it was horrible for me to lose my husband, I cannot imagine the pain of my in-laws losing their son. Yes, he was an adult, but he was and is their boy. While no comparison can be made, I cannot imagine the pain of losing my little boy. I am a widow. Merriam-Webster's Dictionary defines an orphan as a child deprived by death of one or both parents. By that definition, Cole could be considered an orphan. There is no name for a parent who has lost a child. It simply should not happen, but sadly it does. And it naturally leads us to ask why? The biggest why for me was more for Cole; why does Cole have to grow up without his Daddy? Travis wanted nothing more in life than to be a dad. So why did he only get six short months with his boy? Unfortunately, I will never have answers to these questions. Maybe I will in Heaven, but not in my time here.

Some, like me, may also question God. Where were you, God? Why didn't You stop this from happening? I knew God was capable of keeping Travis alive, and I was angry with Him for letting Travis die. I lost track of how many times I questioned God. Never has my faith been so deeply challenged than when I lost Travis. Where was God when he was seizing? Why didn't He stop the seizure? Why did He allow Travis to die? These "whys" will never have any answers for me. In the weeks and months following Travis' death, I had to wrestle with these questions, desperately wanting answers but also knowing I wouldn't get them. That kind of turmoil within one's mind can only be described as a storm of chaos and emotion. Within that storm, I was lashing out at whatever I could. Most often, the target of my raging was God. Luckily for me, God is big enough to handle our tantrums. Many might see this lashing out at God as horrible or sin or something we should never do. I don't think God sees it that way. While I was angry with God, He still had my attention. What I didn't realize at the time was in all my questions, my focus was where it needed to be. My human mind can run circles around these questions, but it will lead to nothing but despair. Maybe you are like me. For months, I lived in that state of despair simply because I could not let go of the why. I had allowed my anger to hijack my faith. Grief is a weird thing when it comes to faith. How does one hold on to faith and trust in God when they have suffered so much pain? How do you trust that God still cares when He took someone so important to us, especially so soon? It is not easy.

Once I realized my anger was only leading to bitterness, I had to find a way to break that cycle. I had to somehow restore the belief that God still cared about me. I had to intentionally remind myself of whom God is, not just what He allows. I don't believe God took Travis from me, but He did allow it to happen. God was capable of stopping it. He could have protected Travis from the seizure. He could have opened Travis' lungs and made him breathe. God could have kept him alive for Cole and me, but He didn't. It seems cruel, doesn't it? To allow someone so young to die, leaving behind a wife and baby? It seems cruel God would allow anyone to die, no matter what age they were or the relationships they had. We get so focused on the unfairness of the circumstances we forget who is in control. It sounds so cliché, doesn't it? Oh, remember, God is in control. Well, if He was in control, why didn't He control the seizure and keep Travis alive? See how easy it is for our brains to circle back to the why? The constant questions of why leave us with nothing but despair and anguish. I think the root of all the whys really boils down to our human nature questioning the goodness of God. How many times in life have you heard someone ask, "Well, if God is so good, why does this or that happen?" Aren't we doing the same thing? If God is so good, why did this person I loved so much have to die?

I think an excellent example of this dichotomy can be seen in the life of Job. Job was a wealthy man with many livestock and servants. He was a righteous man who followed the Lord and turned away from sin. All in all, you could say Job was a good person. Then, right when everything in Job's life seemed to be going well, he lost it all. All his children were killed, along with his livestock. All his land was destroyed. His life went from plentiful and joyful to empty and devastating with no warning. Sounds familiar, doesn't it? Whether your loved one was sick for a long time or it was an unexpected loss, your life still completely changed the moment he or she passed. Like us, Job lamented the loss of his family and property. Job describes his and our pain well in Job 30.

> "The night racks my bones, and the pain that gnaws me takes no rest... God has cast me into the mire, and I have become like dust and ashes. I cry to you for help and you do not answer me..." (Job 30: 17, 19-20)

I don't know about you, but I can definitely identify with the agony described in just a few short verses. The pain that does not cease, the betrayal of loss, the feeling of abandonment. For several chapters,

Job rants against God. But again, God is big enough to handle even the worst of our ravings. Job did have one advantage, though: a friend willing to remind him of truth. Elihu spends several chapters speaking to Job of God's greatness. Of course, Job didn't want to hear that in the middle of his circumstances. He ranted and raved for a bit but eventually went silent. In the silence, God was there. When Job was willing to let go of his anger and questions, God restored his life. For Job, that was a restoration of wealth and prosperity. Job 42:12 says, "And the Lord blessed the latter days of Job more than his beginning..." While our loved ones will not be restored to us, we can be given the peace and joy we so desperately need. Although our lives may look different than we wanted, it doesn't mean our lives are destroyed. You can find joy in life again as you learn to move forward without your loved one beside you.

I will never understand why Travis was taken from me so soon or why Cole has to grow up without his Daddy. It took me a long time to accept this, but I don't think I am meant to understand. Beth Moore,

15

an American evangelist, author and Bible teacher, wrote, "Sometimes we stand to learn the most about God from situations we understand the least."[2] Maybe that's what this is about. I can say I have felt a peace beyond comprehension through this pain. Yes, it is still painful. To an extent, it always will be. What I have learned is the only way to survive this pain is to remember who God is, not just what He allows. From this pain, I can easily call God my rock, my hope, my strength. I don't know if I could have said that before Travis died.

In a study on the life of David, I have realized how much David truly suffered. He was hunted. He grieved the loss of many friends, most specifically his closest friends Uzzah and Jonathon. But David knew something few people truly understand, that I am only beginning to understand myself: with God, devastation can always lead to celebration. Beth Moore wrote, "Devastation when we expect celebration is almost more than we can take."[2] I can't think of a better way to describe the utter emptiness that followed Travis' death. I expected to

16

spend my life with him. I expected to watch him play with Cole and teach him everything he knew. When what you expect is so suddenly and unexpectedly ripped away, there is a feeling that cannot be described. To one who has not experienced such intense grief, it is almost unimaginable. To those who have experienced it like I have, there is no way to adequately express everything that comes with it. Grief is sadness, anger, grief, misery, betrayal, confusion, fear, and so much more all rolled into one.

I once heard someone describe grief as a tornado. I have found it is only within the chaos of the winds, rain, and darkness can we truly understand the peace and comfort of God. Peace that passes understanding mentioned in Philippians 4:7 is only a Christian catchphrase until you find yourself in the midst of it. Whether it was a conscious decision or not (I'm still not really sure), I depended on God (and several key individuals) for a long time. I still do. In all my rants against God, I didn't realize I was doing myself a favor by focusing

17

on Him. Over time, I began to accept I will not, nor do I really need the answers to my whys. Once I allowed myself to release my grip on the need for answers, I learned the only thing I could really place my focus was on God. Only by keeping my focus on God through struggle and pain have I truly learned what it means to say, "It is well."[3]

Reflections

1. What are your "why" questions? Why do you think you want those answers?

2. In what ways can you relate to Job? Try to look deeper than just relating to his pain.

3. How do you think you can relate to David?

Perspectives: Maryellen

What were the circumstances of your loss?

I did not see it coming. Maybe I should have. Within 45 minutes my life and the lives of my three children changed forever. My husband Bill had struggled with asthma for years, but we thought he had it under control. One morning as I was taking my daughter to school Bill was not able to breathe and called 911. I returned to a bunch of First Responders pounding at my door and Bill unresponsive. They were not able to revive him. I had lost the love of my life, the amazing father of my children, my best friend, my life as I knew it and my future. I was cast into a world of uncertainty, indescribable pain and a level of deep, deep sadness I had never known, and had no control over.

Can you describe your faith prior to the loss?

I have always been a faithful person. I would not say outwardly religious or evangelistic, but more private. I always felt that the way I practiced my faith was through my love and service to others. I trusted in God, but the bottom line was I was the one in control and God alongside me, helping to guide me, but really I was OK by myself or with my happy little family and world as it was.

Can you describe your faith in the time after the loss?

When Bill passed I felt I had lost everything. I would try to be grateful for what I had and look at what was still the same in my world. I had lost all control of my world. I had lost "my person", and as much as people helped I really had nobody. My Mom had passed a few years prior and my Dad quite awhile ago. I had nobody who was always there exactly when I needed them. Except God. I did not understand why this all happened to me and my children. I cannot say that I was never angry at God. I wondered why He caused hurt and suffering over and over again in the world. But more than being angry with Him, I needed Him. Often my prayer was "God, get me through the next five minutes pleeeeeaaaasssee!" I began to rely on Him to get me through the days, weeks and months. I taped up on my wall so that I could read several times per day the bible verse "Trust in the Lord with all your heart and lean not on your own understanding" Proverbs 3:5

In what ways did you feel your faith was challenged due to loss?

My relationship with God has changed and become deeper. Faith and prayer has become not just something to have as part of my daily routine, but an actual need. It gives me the Peace that I cannot find in any other way. I no longer really question the "why" that this all happened, but have great Faith that God has a plan in this for me and for my children. In some ways we have all grown in ways that absolutely would not have happened without losing Bill. I have seen times where it can only be God's hand in directing my family a certain way. There have been several incidents where something happens and I know God made it happen. Don't get me wrong; we have been through two years of very tough struggles and challenges. Many times the answer to my prayer has been "wait" – and I'm not a patient person! It's just that there is Peace about me now. If I give that control to God, I know He will carry me in the direction He wants me to go! Prayer time and church time has become a "need" and refills my soul more than it ever has before!

What do you wish you had known about grief?

When you hear of someone passing, you are saddened and feel horrible for the family. But as an outsider you have absolutely have no idea of the level of pain and sadness. I am glad I knew nothing about grief. If someone had told me what it was like, I would have thought, I'm tough, I can handle anything. I'll be sad, but I'll handle it. How wrong I would have been.

What has helped or hindered your healing?

Honestly, as much as I love my children, watching them grieve and helping them work through their pain has added an additional element. At times, just when I thought I had made a small amount of progress one of the children would come crashing down! When your children hurt, as a parent you hurt for them. After two years, I truly feel we are stronger for it, but it has been a very rocky road for sure!

What is your greatest word of advice for those who are suffering grief and loss?

My advice is to remain in the present. Your mind is all over the board! It is so easy to go back to the "would have, could have, should have". It's just as easy to worry about the future and what am I going to do for the rest of my life. To survive I have had to train my mind to stay in the present. When I would look too far out I would say to myself "You're not there yet." A lot of self-talk, and talking to God to just get me through the "now."

The Okay Trap

Imagine this scenario: You are having a conversation with a friend, acquaintance, or family member. Inevitably, the question comes up. "How are you doing?" What would your answer be? More often than not, your answer would be something along the lines of "I'm okay." Those of us in grief often use this phrase to deflect any uncomfortable conversation. If we are truly honest, we are not okay. We are really not okay in the first six months or so; at least I wasn't. Of course, those months are when you will hear this question all the time. I think I was asked this question in almost every single conversation for the first three months. Inevitably, my answer was always some variation of "okay." After a few months of this, people stopped asking. Sure, some of my closest friends and family would still ask here and there, but it definitely wasn't as often.

I remember being angry with people. I would have a conversation with a friend, and they would not ask how I was. After the conversation ended, I would be offended or indignant. How could my friend not check on me? Don't they want to make sure I'm okay? After months of this, I just accepted that no one cared anymore. But that was not the case! Of course my friends still cared about me. Of course they want me to be doing well. For months, I kept telling them I was fine, so they started treating me as if I was. I had returned to work and was taking care of Cole. I repeatedly told them I was okay. From their perspective, I was doing well. What they couldn't see, or I wouldn't allow them to see, was I

26

was not doing very well. Sure, I was moving through life as a relatively functional adult, but I definitely was not fine. When we continually tell people we are okay, they will start to believe us. Yes, their actions are their own, and maybe you think they should be checking in on you more often. Maybe they don't ask anymore because they believe you are doing well and don't want to upset you.

American culture does not know how to handle grief. Most people think asking how a grieving person is doing will remind the person of the grief. Well, it's not like we forgot. I don't go about living my life until someone comes along, asks how I'm doing, and I suddenly remember Travis died. That's just not how it works. Yet, for whatever reason, that's what people think. Sometimes people don't ask about your grief because they don't want to deal with their own emotions. Most people don't know what to say to someone who is grieving, so they don't say anything at all. Whatever the reason may be, it can sometimes be hurtful to the griever when their friends or family don't ask how they are doing.

It is easy for us to become angry with people or start to think they don't care. More often than not, I think people don't ask out of fear of causing more pain, or they just genuinely believe you are doing well. While it may be difficult not to have someone checking on you, I don't think it is fair of us to get angry. Again, they are responsible for their own actions, but when we continually lie and say we are okay, eventually, they will believe us.

I call this phenomenon the Okay Trap. As grievers, we can get so focused on pretending to be okay we unintentionally drive away some of our greatest supporters. Maybe we are trying to hold it together for the sake of others. Perhaps you lost a spouse, but you are trying to keep yourself together for the sake of your child who lost a parent. In my case, Cole was too young to understand his Daddy was gone. I was trying to hold myself together for the sake of my mother-in-law. We have always had, and still have a very good relationship. For a long time, neither of us really talked about Travis, at least not to each other. Both of us were afraid to upset the other. I still talked about Travis with my family and a couple of friends, but never to her. Honestly, I mentioned him a few times, but as soon as I would say his name, she would start to cry. This is understandable, but I just couldn't deal with it. I remember getting frustrated that I couldn't even ask a question about his headstone without upsetting her. I had to remind myself she was grieving too. We are so easily angered or upset by people while we are grieving. This is a natural reaction, and I don't think there is anything wrong with that. However, we do ourselves and everyone else a favor when we give people a little bit of grace. When you are hurting, it can be so difficult but I think it is necessary to some extent. No, people won't always say the right things. Sometimes what they say, even if it is well-meant, can be hurtful. In most cases, people will not say or do anything to intentionally cause you more pain.

Now, you've probably already heard some of these hurtful comments. Maybe they were the generic "they're in a better place now," or "now you have an angel watching over you." Not only are these not at all helpful, but they can be straight-up painful. For me, some of the worst ones were typical Christian-ese sayings. "God never gives anyone more than they can handle" was my least favorite. Really? God thought I could easily handle becoming a widow and single mom at 29? Or my in-laws could handle losing their son? I was paralyzed after Travis died. I couldn't take care of myself and definitely couldn't take care of my son. It was like people thought losing my husband was equivalent to losing my favorite hoodie. I'd think, "Nope, but thanks for writing off my pain as something that I can just handle on my own." One thing I learned really quick was God definitely allows more than we can handle! I also learned (as soon as I got out of the fog of the initial shock) when we are given more than we can handle, there is only one way to handle it: trust God.

Reflections

1. How do you respond when people ask how you are doing?

2. Have you noticed any change in how others treat you as time has passed?

3. One strategy to avoid the okay trap is to answer based solely on that day. For instance, "I am doing okay today," or "Today has been rough." Do you think this strategy may help you avoid the trap? Can you think of any other ways to avoid the okay trap?

Perspectives: Ellie

What were the circumstances of your loss?

My mother had been diagnosed with Chronic Lymphocytic Leukemia (CLL) in 2002. She was 44. Over the next seven years, she battled the disease. It seemed like every six months she relapsed and was back on chemotherapy of some type. She spent much of her times in remission battling infections that were the result of a compromised immune system. My youngest daughter was born in November of 2007, my mom was able to come visit us in the hospital. But by Christmas, she had fallen pretty ill. Her immune system was so out of whack that she started having all sorts of problems - shingles, gall bladder issues, body rashes. She spent the first part of 2008 bedridden due to her illnesses. In Spring of 2008, things started looking up. She felt good. Her faith was revitalized. She was able to attend church and family events. In early Fall, her health started to falter again. Her oncologist indicated that it was time for the "hail Mary" - a bone marrow transplant. For the type of Leukemia she had, at that time, this was the final option for treatment. She'd exhausted all the chemotherapies that were effective. She had her consultation on October 31. The specialist said he needed her to spend some time getting healthy. However, she continued to get weaker. For some reason, I had a hard time seeing this for what it was at the time and remained optimistic. She went into the hospital at the beginning of December and remained there until after Christmas. On the day after Christmas, we received a call from an Infectious Disease doctor and her oncologist. Her cancer was active AND an infection was rampant at the same time. They couldn't fight both at the same time and therefore there was nothing they could do but put her into Hospice care. I had a hard time accepting this at the time. I think it was a matter of "not seeing the forest for the trees." She passed away at home on January 10, 2008. I was beside her as she took her last breath.

Can you describe your faith prior to the loss?

My faith was strong at the time of her death. I was a pastor's wife and had just recently been encouraged by my mother's own steps of faith. She struggled with her own faith during her illness - about eight months before her death, my daughter (four years old at the time), told my mom that "a girl should have her grandma and grandpa at church with her." My mom came back to church and renewed her relationship with the Lord.

Can you describe your faith in the time after the loss?

 I never really struggled with my faith, per se. But I really struggled with all the stories about how God had brought about good through the death of others' loved ones. I hadn't experienced that. My dad walked away from faith after my mother passed (still to this day has not returned). And my brother renounced belief in God altogether (and shared this with my mom on her death bed). I was pretty depressed for months afterward. I felt ripped off because I was 32 when she died - and my kids were 4 and 1. I knew they'd never remember her and I'd never have those "mother/daughter/granddaughter" things. I'd be out in public and see women my age out to lunch with their own mothers and their daughters, and I'd break down crying. It wasn't until years later that I was able to find some "good." My own daughter was struggling with if she hears from God or if God uses her...we shared the story of her telling my mom essentially to come back to faith and that strengthened her faith.

In what ways did you feel your faith was challenged due to loss?

It was at this time that I learned to become comfortable sharing my ugly feelings with God. My anger over the situation, my anger at Him. I never liked "complaining" to God before this. I always felt like my complaints were trite because He had bigger things to deal with. I didn't know what else to do but bring them to Him because I was determined to not let my own grief/depression affect mothering of my kids. (My mom lost her mom when my brother and I were teenagers - she kind of checked out at that point for a few years while she processed her grief. I didn't want to do that.

What do you wish you had known about grief?

That there are no "shoulds." You "should" be at this point by now. You "shouldn't" feel like this at this point. Etc.

What has helped or hindered your healing?

My husband was very supportive during this time. He shouldered a lot of burdens for me and was very patient and kind. Hindered: I've never really been able to talk about deep, significant things with my dad and brother. So our discussions of grief and faith have been fairly non-existent through this time.

What is your greatest word of advice for those who are suffering grief and loss?

People generally won't know what to say or do to help you - unless they've experienced loss themselves. Don't hold that against them or get upset when they say something "thoughtless." Also, everyone else will get back to their "real lives" and you'll be stuck for a while. This will be very difficult. You'll feel like everyone has forgotten your grief. But do your best to not get upset with people for moving on.

Love Redefined

If you are like me, you might have heard it said grief is a love that no longer has a place to belong. I wholeheartedly disagree. Honestly, when I first heard the concept, it was in an article on Facebook. I truly had a physical reaction to what I believed to be a horrid idea. I was appalled anyone could believe my love didn't belong anymore. Grief is not a love that no longer has a place to belong. At least not to me.

My love and heart will always belong to Travis. He will always be my love, and he will always be Daddy to Cole. My love has not changed simply because Travis is no longer physically here with me. The only thing that has changed is how that love is expressed. I can't kiss him or hold his hand. I miss the snuggles. I miss the morning and goodnight kisses every day. Just because we no longer have those physical expressions of love doesn't mean our love for this person is somehow displaced. One of my favorite songs related to my grief is Switchfoot's "What It Cost." The song speaks to the relationship between love and loss. One of the lines is "love is the currency of loss." Just because loss happens doesn't mean love no longer exists. It is simply exchanged for another expression of that love.

Since Travis' death, I show my love for him in new ways. I express my love in how I raise Cole. Others may light a candle or start a tradition to remember and honor their loved one. There is no right or wrong way to express love for a passed loved one. It could be something as simple as talking to him or her, even knowing no answer will come. It could be a starting a new tradition. In my situation, I wanted to make Father's Day a special day. Travis always wanted to be a dad. He only had one Father's Day, but he was as proud as I had ever seen him. I gave him a Dad shirt, and he wore it gladly. Because it was such a special day for Travis, I wanted to keep it a special day. Travis loved fishing, so I came up with a plan. There is a large metro park and lake near me that we had fished before. For Father's Day, I got my parents and my in-laws to go with Cole and me to fish this lake. We spent most of the day sitting in lawn chairs on the edge of the water. Sometimes we would talk, sometimes not. Did I have to walk away a few times? Yes. And that's okay. Someone who suffered devastating loss as I have may start a tradition or come up with an idea that can be a challenge. It's okay to walk away for a little bit. I left my family and walked farther down the shore to have a good cry. Whatever you do, enjoy it as much as you can, and give yourself the freedom to cry if you need to.

The same article I mentioned earlier also suggested grief is not a loss. Um, what?! Grief is very much a loss to anyone who has experienced it. The death of my husband was a significant loss in my life. I lost the hugs and kisses I would get every day. I lost the laugh and smile I so much enjoyed. I lost the life I expected to live with him. I once heard it said that grief is an assault on our expectations. I expected to grow old with him. I expected to watch Travis teach Cole how to build and fix things. I lost that opportunity. Cole has lost the chance to see his Daddy smile at every milestone he has made and will reach in his life. He lost the chance to hear his Daddy say, "I'm proud of you," or "I love you." Yes, he heard these things when Travis was alive, but he will not remember them. He was too young. Death of a loved one is very much a loss. Not only in that moment, but in all the missed opportunities that follow.

If you have suffered loss, I'm sure you can think of some missed opportunities. Perhaps you are young and have lost a parent. That parent may not have lived to see your wedding or the birth of your children. If you lost a child, your difficult losses might be a birthday or when the child would have graduated. Perhaps you are grieving a child you didn't get the opportunity to meet. Your missed opportunity may be the birth of this child. I don't say this to be depressing; I say it to show there are so many missed opportunities. But we can turn these missed opportunities into something special too. I don't get to see Travis enjoy another Father's Day, but I will see Cole enjoy Father's Day with his Papa and Papaw doing something Travis loved. If you can, try to find a way to turn the sadness of missed opportunities into moments to joy in remembering your loved one.

Reflections

1. What can you identify as missed opportunities?

2. If you have already experienced some of these missed opportunities, how did you handle them?

3. For future missed opportunities, what ideas can you think of to help you find joy in those moments?

Perspectives: Kim and Bill

What were the circumstances of your loss?

Our daughter Nicole was in active labor at the hospital. Preceding her second push, she had a brain aneurysm.

Can you describe your faith prior to your loss?

Very strong that Jesus is our Savior.

Can you describe your faith in the time after your loss?

Our faith sustained our family. He was every breath we took.

In what ways did you feel your faith was challenged due to loss?

Our faith was not challenged at all. We were very grateful we have the Holy Spirit and Friends to pray.

What has helped or hindered your healing?

What has helped: Connecting with other friends that have lost a child, attending a support group called grief share, and knowing that she is with the Lord. One day we will be together again, this is not our home.

What has hindered: Nothing.

What is your greatest word of advice for those who are suffering grief and loss?

Attend a support group. One major help for me was to learn there is no wrong way of grieving. To give ourselves permission to cry, laugh, and cry some more. I learned that my mind would play tricks, thinking that I saw her. Being at the grocery store breaking down after seeing her favorite food.

There's no time frame for healing, time does not heal our pain. Journal.

God's Love in Loss

One thing that never ceases to amaze me is how much God loves us. Yes, I know I got a reaction from you. How could a loving God let this happen? Please hear me out. Jesus came to earth for the sole purpose of sacrificing Himself so we could know Him. Yes, I would gladly give my life to spare Cole's, but I think any mother would say the same. If you lost a child, I can only imagine how many times you might have thought, "if only I could take his/her place." For me, it was "if only I had been home to give him his medicine, maybe I could have saved him." These are the thoughts of our own humanity. Nothing is wrong with them, but God's thoughts are very different. Instead of trying to save His only Son, He sent Him to earth to die for me. For Cole. For you. For everyone. Even the one we might consider to be the epitome of evil.

What human could say that? That I would send my only child, my son, to die a horribly brutal and painful death to save a total stranger, let alone one whom most people would consider not worthy of saving. Let's be honest here: how easy is it for us to say, "the world is better off" or "he deserved it" when a child molester is murdered in prison? Pretty easy for us, isn't it? But these deaths and losses grieve God greatly. He loves every soul on earth. Even the serial rapists or child molesters who can be so difficult (for us) to even care about, let alone want a relationship with. That's why Jesus willingly walked to the shackles of the Romans, knowing it would lead to a death so unimaginably painful. But Jesus was also human; He knew what must happen to allow us to have a relationship with Him, but He wasn't looking forward to it.

Jesus' apprehension is evident in the Garden of Gethsemane. Jesus told his disciples in Matthew 26:38, "My soul is overwhelmed with sorrow." Jesus knew what was coming that night. He left his disciples, walking a bit farther into the garden, and desperately prayed for His Father to make another way. With increasing anguish, Jesus prayed, "Father, everything is possible with You. Take this cup from me" (Mark 14:36). Can you imagine? Knowing the level of pain and suffering you were about to endure? Any of us would be begging God to spare us, and even Jesus did. He prayed that prayer three times before being betrayed. Jesus said in Matthew 26:42, "My Father, if it is not possible for this cup to be taken away unless I drink it, may Your will be done." Even in the face of such suffering, Jesus was willing. He was prepared to die a traitor's death so you and I (and the murderer and the rapist and the cheater) could be saved. Such a love is incomprehensible.

While Jesus' sacrifice was the ultimate display of love and compassion, God shows us love in other ways too. God so intimately knows each and every person, and He will show His love in the exact way that person needs. For me, the greatest display of God's love came after Travis died. To the human mind, that thought is illogical. How could God's love be displayed in the loss of my husband, whom I love? While I will never know why he had to die, I also don't know what he was spared from. Perhaps his death was an act of mercy for him. Maybe there were other things in his future that would have been too painful for Travis to bear. Maybe his death, while painful for me, was the greatest thing God could do for Travis. Let's be honest; Travis is doing just fine in Heaven. I am sure he was upset and disappointed to leave Cole and me so soon, but we will see him again. It will only be an instant for Travis before we are in Heaven as well. What joy is it to know that Travis may have been spared from suffering with such mercy that only God can show? Isn't mercy an act of love as well? As counterintuitive as it may seem, Travis' death could have been an act of mercy, and thus love to Travis. But then there's me. And my in-laws. And everyone else who loved Travis. You may ask, as I did many times, where is God in this pain of loss? I came to find out God was right there with me in every moment of grief, and will remain with me for as long as I allow Him. How else could I explain the peace I have felt? That peace is as illogical as Travis' death being an act of mercy, but both peace and mercy flow from love. I think God allows other things to be so I can feel peace and joy in this loss.

It can be difficult to see God in times of pain. I cannot explain God's love in your specific situation. I can only point you in the right direction. The only way I was able to see the love and mercy in my loss was by asking for it. It sounds cliché, but ask God to show you His love. He will show you His love if you are willing to listen. One verse I have come to cherish in the months following Travis' death is Psalm 36:7

51

"How precious is Your steadfast love, O God! The children of mankind take refuge in the shadow of Your wings." Steadfast. I don't know if I could describe God's love in a single word better than David did in this verse. Steadfast love is constant, devoted, good, steady, and true. We can take refuge in His love, as I have done since Travis' death. Refuge is a beautiful word as well, and we don't use it often. Refuge means a shelter or protection from danger or distress. In refuge, we can have peace. Thanks to God's unfailing love, we both can rest peacefully in His protection. What a beautifully comforting notion of love.

Reflections

1. In what ways do you feel you can relate to Jesus' anguish in the garden?

2. Can you identify ways God has shown His love to you? If you are struggling to see it, that's okay. It took me a long time to be able to see it, too.

3. Take time to reflect on Psalm 36:7. What comfort can you find in those words?

Perspectives: GC

GC lost her dad at a young age

What were the circumstances of your loss?

Unexpected. Caught me off-guard.

Can you describe your faith prior to the loss?

I was (and still am) a Christ-Follower. Describing it in terms of human development, I would say I was teenager in the Lord. I was blessed to have, fairly recently, formed a pretty good foundation, however I was still very green. I still have much to learn.

Can you describe your faith in the time after the loss?

My relationship with Him grew tremendously. I had no choice but to lean in, all in, to my Lord. He was, and is, and always will be my Rock. He truly became my Father. I had to rely more than ever on my Lord to provide for me, to protect me, to care for me.

Also note that I had to make that choice.

In what ways did you feel your faith was challenged due to loss?

I think I would rather say that I was tested to see if I would choose God. I had to live out what I claimed I believed.

What do you wish you had known about grief?

Grief was brand new to me. God blessed me with great teachers to teach me along the way. I remember someone sharing with me, like a heads-up, that grief will randomly hit you. One person, who was maybe in her fifties, shared that she had lost her dad a number of years prior, and that sometimes she still sobs at his grave all these years later. Others had also reassured me along the way, and advised me how to handle that. Having that woman give me that "heads-up" was huge. It helped me understand the random and intense longings I sometimes get. Also note, they sometimes come at inopportune times.

What is your greatest word of advice for those who are suffering grief and loss?

If you haven't chosen the Lord yet, please choose Him. He is waiting. If you have chosen the Lord, continue to choose Him. Run to Him again and again. There's a song that goes something like that. The Lord makes the biggest difference. He is faithful and has proven Himself so to me. He is the One who walked me through the whole process... and still walks with me. He never leaves. He is the One who comforts.

Blessing in Pain

One of the easiest ways I can see God's love during this pain is to look for the blessings, no matter how small they may be. I will give you some of the ones I have found in my story to help those of you suffering loss find some of yours. I have heard many times, as you likely have as well if you grew up in church, that God's timing is perfect. It doesn't seem that way when your husband dies at such a young age, leaving a six-month-old son to grow up without him, but we do not know why Travis was taken from us. Maybe it really was mercy. Looking back on the past few years, I can see how God has worked some things out for me. I never wanted kids. Travis wanted nothing more in life than to be a dad, yet married me, knowing I didn't want to be a mom. My mind changed a few years ago after watching Travis play with and love our nephew. Once we decided to start trying for a baby, it did not take long. I do not say this to brag, as I know many who have struggled with the pain of infertility but hear me out. We started trying in August, and I got pregnant at the end of September. It can take a year for a healthy young couple to get pregnant, yet God blessed us after only a month. Cole was due June 28, but God doesn't always listen to the medical world. Cole came early, at only 35 weeks, but was generally healthy. We had a short 4-day NICU stay, but no breathing problems at all. Breathing issues are to be expected for a 35-weeker, but God developed Cole's lungs sooner than most so we could go home. I questioned God at the time, "why did Cole come early? Why should I have to leave him alone in NICU overnight?"

Knowing what I know now, I am grateful for the five extra weeks Cole had with his Daddy. If Cole had not been early, Travis would have never had a Father's Day. I will forever cherish the moments and photos from that day. Travis was so proud to be a dad, and he loved every second of it (well, maybe not getting up in the middle of the night). Travis was not only blessed with a Father's Day, but he almost didn't get to meet Cole at all. Travis had a long history of seizures, starting when he was very young. There had been many instances in which he stopped breathing. He had had one of these seizures in January, but I was home to give him his medicine to bring him out of the seizure and breathe again. He could have easily died then had I not been there or if the medicine had not worked. He was also in a bad car accident in February that almost totaled his brand new car, but he walked away with nothing but some bruises. God spared Travis from these (and maybe some we don't know about) to allow him to enjoy his son, even if only for six months. While I don't know everything, I do know this: God is merciful and loving. He has displayed this to me on several occasions; I just have to be willing to see it.

Those who are suffering may be struggling to see how God's love and mercy show in your situation. Someone in pain might be trying to see it for months, but can't seem to find that small light inside the darkness. Anyone who has experienced grief understands the darkness that can surround you. While you walk in daylight, the heart and mind are surrounded by the black night of grief. You can see the light of the physical world around you, but the night of grief in your soul will not allow you to see past your pain. It is sometimes hard to believe the pain and darkness will ever fade. Over time, and with some work, the darkness slowly recedes into the distance. It is always there, but with God's mercy, it can recede enough to allow your heart to feel joy again. For me, the best way to help push back the darkness is to focus on God's blessings. Even if you can find one tiny detail to thank God for, it is a start. Maybe you can be thankful for the voicemail you saved so you can hear their voice. If you lost a child, you might be thankful for the stuffed animal or blanket they found comfort in. May it be of some comfort to you as well if you still have it. Maybe it is a video of his or her smile and laugh. Whatever you are able to find, focus on it, and thank God for it. As you do this, you will see more and more blessings the darkness has been hiding from you. The blessings won't take away the pain, but they can lighten the burden, even if only for a few moments.

Reflections

1. I found comfort in the timing of Cole's birth. Is there some evidence of timing you can find comfort in?

2. Is there a more tangible comfort, like a child's stuffed animal or a saved voicemail?

3. Are there any blessings you have already identified?

Perspectives: Rachel

What were the circumstances of your loss?

We lost Travis suddenly and very unexpectedly. He was my brother-in-law, my younger sister's husband, and he was only 29 years old when he died. I was walking into work on a Tuesday in November, running a little late and hands full. It's not unusual for me to hear from my mom in the morning so I wasn't at all alarmed when she called, but I was still trying to make my way into the building and didn't want to wrestle my phone from my purse as I was juggling multiple bags so I just thought I'd call her back once I'd reached my office. My anxiety spiked a bit when she called again immediately. This is universal code for bad news, right? I answered and my stomach sank when I heard she was crying. Of course I start to panic, my mind racing through family members. When she said it, I remember I froze mid-step, in the middle of the building lobby in disbelief. Once I willed my feet to move again, I headed for my office - faster now - to dump the bags and try to get my head to stop spinning. After talking to mom for a few minutes and arguing with her that I was okay to drive, I told my boss I had to go and headed back to my car.

Since my sister and I are very close, my husband and I spent a lot of time with her and Travis. They were the first ones we called for double dates, concerts, and hangouts. Our default people. I was in complete shock as I called my husband, dropping the bomb on him right before the start of his day, and started the hour and a half drive south to their house. I had been pretty determined not to cry at work and to just get things done and get out as fast as possible. But now, in the car alone, there was no holding back anymore. I screamed and sobbed as I drove. I was devastated and heartbroken, of course, but I was also furious. How could God do this? How could He take Travis from Sara and their 6-month old baby? From his parents and brother? From us all? The injustice of it was too much. And so I raged.

Can you describe your faith prior to the loss?

I was in a pretty solid place in my faith before we lost Trav. I was active in my church and faith disciplines, in spite of earlier losses. About a year before Travis died, my grandmother had passed away right before Christmas and on my wedding anniversary. While the holiday lost a lot of it's joy that year, I had handled that loss okay all things considered. She had experienced many health issues in the years leading up to her death, so even though selfishly I would have kept her here forever, I could strain to glimpse the mercy in it when God took her home. But Trav's death brought on a totally different reaction.

Can you describe your faith in the time after the loss?

My faith was decimated when we lost Travis. To hold my baby sister and cry with her and watch her grieve the loss of her husband of only a few years? Unacceptable. To rock my sweet nephew and mourn his loss that he couldn't yet understand?

Unbearable. How dare He? One of my most vivid memories in the days following Trav's death was going with Sara and our families to make all the arrangements. As moral support, or so I thought. Instead, I found myself reeling, silently and continuously struggling to find my bearings and keep my anger in check. What right did I even have to be angry when his widow (and my baby sister) was standing nearby, making these heart-wrenching decisions? How could my pain even begin to compare to the loss his mother was navigating? So I kept my fury to myself, and tried to support Sara in whatever tangible and practical ways I could. Anything to keep my mind and my hands busy. One moment that stands out in particular was in the funeral home when Sara and the family were selecting a casket. I will never forget having to walk away for a moment, hands shaking, furiously text my inner circle of friends to keep from screaming at the top of my lungs. "I just don't know how my faith is going to recover from this one, guys," I wrote. And if I'm honest, I'm still working on it.

In what ways did you feel your faith was challenged due to loss?

Losing Travis hit at the absolute foundation of what I believed about God: That He is good. That He is merciful. That He is in control. That He is trustworthy. Because in the middle of my grief, where life felt too sad and unjust and entirely out of control, I could not fathom that any of this experience was compatible with the God I had envisioned. This affront to my core beliefs about God challenged the whole of my faith, because if He wasn't good after all, what was I even doing following Him? And how could I ever believe that He was good again if this was acceptable to Him? How could I believe in His mercy when it had been withheld from Travis and our family? If He was truly in control, then why had He not prevented this? And most of all, how could I possibly trust Him when this is where He brought us?

I wouldn't say that I turned my back on God during this season, as I still wanted to believe and worked hard to choose faith over my emotions. But it wasn't pretty. "Ready to pick another fight with you today, God," I would begin. And then I'd let it all out. During the first few weeks, I spent a lot of time on the road driving to Sara's, and this turned out to be a helpful processing time. To me, it was prayer. Not terribly reverent prayer to be blunt, but it was all I had in me at the time. I'd tell Him how furious and heartbroken I was. Sometimes crying, sometimes screaming, almost always brutally honest with wherever my emotions had me that day. And amazingly enough, I found He listened. In my rage, He stilled my heart. In my sadness, He wrapped His inexplicable peace around me. And thus, we started to rebuild my faith together. Day by day, or moment by moment if necessary, but I threw it all at Him and I found that He did not shy away from it. I brought the angriest, ugliest, and most bitter parts of me to these prayers, and like the loving Father I have once again found Him to be, He simply listened and didn't shy away from how my pain and grief showed up. I will never understand why God allowed this loss on this side of eternity, but I also no longer view it as a deal-breaker to my faith. I have come back to a genuine belief that God is good, and merciful, and in control, and trustworthy. It has been a process to be sure, and one I still grapple with sometimes. But we are back on our way, and I feel like that is what matters most.

What do you wish you had known about grief?

I have experienced other losses where my grief appeared in more expected ways (at least more in line with my expectations anyway), such as sadness or discouragement. But what I wish I had known about grief was that anger is an entirely valid and acceptable emotion. In fact, I wish I had known that anything that I may or may not be feeling in processing my grief or loss is valid. Attempting to conform to my expectations of what loss and grief look like would not be helpful or productive. I also wish I had known that there would be both expected and unexpected hard times. Milestones,

71

anniversaries, birthdays, Father's Day, Christmas... These are all expected and understandably hard. But the random song on the radio? That one can knock the wind out of me because I can't see it coming. Or another time, a happy thought that "we should come back here with Sara and Trav! He would love it" before my brain reminds me that he's gone? Oof. Those moments are hard and can hit without warning. I wish I had known that these will spring up, not to live in anticipation, but to allow myself more grace when it inevitably happens.

What has helped or hindered your healing?

Because I'd rather end on a positive, I'm going to start with what hindered my healing:

- People can say some truly unhelpful and hurtful things. It took all I had not to unload my anger on people who insisted this was "part of God's plan," "he's in a better place," or some other misguided cliché because they don't know what else to say. Worse yet, when someone would remark to me that at least my sister is young and that she will "find someone else" was deeply upsetting, as if Travis could somehow be replaced. Even if she does choose to remarry some day, this isn't some kind of solution for the pain of this loss.

- I struggled with how quickly everyone seemed to stop talking about Travis. I can intellectually rationalize this response, as I know people may be uncomfortable or grieving in their own way; still, it is hard to feel like he was erased from the narrative or like we are the only ones still missing him.

- My own expectations have probably been the most significant barrier. How I actually processed my grief looked very different than I expected it would, and evolved as time passed. Having fewer expectations of myself across the board would have been healthier and much wiser.

These are some of the things that most helped me in my healing:

- Trusted and non-judgemental friends who were willing to listen without trying to "help." Especially as a verbal-processor who needs to talk things out, I needed a listening ear, not advice. Additionally, I didn't want to process my pain or survivor's guilt with family members who were navigating their own grief, so finding and trusting these few precious friends was a key step.
- An incredibly flexible and understanding supervisor made such a huge difference, as I was able to focus on my family and my healing instead of feeling pressured about work commitments.
- The New Hope Center for Grief Support's 8-week "From Grief to New Hope" Workshop

taught me so much about grief and allowed me to vocalize some of my struggles with a small group in similar loss situations. Finding a specialized grief support network was extremely helpful, both for available resources and the community it offered.

- Most of all, I began to notice what I dubbed "glimpses of grace." These were ways that I saw God coming through for Sara or other family members in the midst of our pain. Friends and family provided for Sara's needs in tangible ways, and this helped me to regain my perception of a good and trustworthy God.

What is your greatest word of advice for those who are suffering grief and loss?

Feel what you feel, as deeply as you feel it. Don't try to minimize your pain or grief, no matter how it shows up. Allow yourself loads of grace as you navigate this loss. (And while you're at it, allow loads of grace for those around you who are also grieving. Just because they don't show their pain in the same way doesn't mean they aren't hurting.)

At the same time, do not wholly trust your emotions. They may be deep and often overwhelming, but they do not always lead to truth. Find a trusted friend, therapist, or pastor to help you navigate your loss in a healthy way, and with no expectation of timeline. Make sure this is someone you feel free to be brutally honest with, as no one ever processed loss or grief by sugar-coating the pain or pretending to be okay when they were not okay.

The Power of Music

Sometimes it can be difficult to remind ourselves of God's love and goodness in times of darkness and pain. During these moments, I turn to music. I have always enjoyed music, so this was natural to me, but if you have suffered a loss and not tried this, I have a list of songs that were helpful to me in the appendix. I encourage you to listen to whatever music you find comfort in. For me, that music is usually worship music. Sometimes, the most important songs can seem to come out of nowhere. There was a night awhile back where I just randomly woke up. There was no discernable reason for me to be awake, but I was. I had Pandora playing, and the first thing I hear is the opening verse of Sovereign Over Us[4]

> "There is strength within the sorrow
> There is beauty in our tears
> And You meet us in the darkness
> With a love that casts out fear
> You are working in our waiting
> You are sanctifying us
> When beyond our understanding
> You are teaching us to trust"

This is why I woke up; I needed to be reminded of these words. Many thoughts came when I heard this verse, but I will break down some of them here.

"There is strength within the sorrow." I know what sorrow is, as I'm sure you do as well. I have lived in sorrow for over a year, and only with God's help am I starting to climb my way out of it. Author and Bible instructor Beth Moore spoke of a sorrow so deep you can't be distracted from it.[2] We don't want to make it through it, but God keeps waking us up every morning. Notice this: GOD wakes us up. It is not by our own strength we are able to get up each day. When sorrow and pain run so deep, we can barely stand it, let alone willingly get up and do life. I heard so many times, and maybe many who have suffered loss have as well, "you're so strong." I appreciate the sentiment, but it's not me. What human heart and mind can stand such deep pain and still keep going? Some probably could, but it would take a lot of time and effort. Was I exhausted? Yes. Am I still? Sometimes. I'm not saying sorrow and grief aren't exhausting to those who live in it. What I am saying is this: with God, there is strength within that sorrow that no human heart or mind could ever hope to muster.

"There is beauty in our tears." Oh, the tears. I don't know I would even want to count the times I have cried since Travis died. I can say I have cried more in the last year or so than I have in my entire 29 years before Travis' death. I have cried at home, at work, at a concert, in a store, in my car, and a whole host of random places. I absolutely hate crying. It defies biology, really. No biological reason exists to cry from emotion, but we do it often. Our tears of grief are sentiments of love to the one we have lost. If that isn't love, what is?

"You meet us in our mourning." That's an interesting word to me: mourning. We don't use it very often, do we? By definition, mourning is a deep sorrow over a loss accompanied by action. Someone in mourning might wear black clothing. For me, mourning looked more like struggling to get dressed at all. And what do we need in a time of mourning? To understand that, we have to understand mourning is grief accompanied by some manifestation or action. I struggled to go through basic daily activities, like getting dressed or showering. What should take 10 minutes took 30 or longer simply because I didn't have the energy to do it. I had such raw emotion tearing through my heart and mind I couldn't focus on the simple task of picking a shirt to wear. When you have that much raw emotion, there is only one thing that can soothe it: peace. By human standards, peace amid deep sorrow and mourning is unattainable. It is against everything we think of and know about grief. However, in my darkest times, I felt a level of peace I cannot explain. Whether I asked Him to or not, God gave me a respite from the pain and offered me peace, if even for a moment. I could never describe the comfort that peace brought me, because how can you describe something that doesn't make sense? It truly is a peace that passes understanding.

"With a love that casts out fear." I think one of the worst emotions in grief is fear. My whole world changed in just a moment. There are practical fears: will I be able to keep the house? How will I raise a boy without his dad? Then there are personal fears: fear I will forget his laugh or my heart will be forever damaged. Fear of the day when I heal enough to take off my wedding ring. It's an odd dynamic, really. I wanted to heal, but I also wanted to hold on to my role as his wife. My logical brain knew that role was over, but my heart couldn't accept it yet. My heart feared the day when my logical brain wins. I have since healed enough to take it off, but it was almost a year before I did so. Fear is such a pervasive and, at times, debilitating emotion, but it doesn't have to be. God met me in my mourning and gave me peace, which brought calmness. Fear is simply anxiety about the unknown, right? In all my fear and anxiety, God settled my heart and mind. I had an understanding that despite my fears, I didn't need to know why or what my life would look like. I just had peace knowing we were going to be okay.

"You are working in our waiting; You are sanctifying us." This waking-in-the-middle-of-the-night experience happened several months ago. At the time, I had a sense my story was to be used for a greater purpose. It was a long time before I discovered that purpose was this book. My story was to be used to help others heal, but I did not know it at the time. I don't think I was meant to know it yet. In 1 Samuel 16:1, God gave Samuel one-step directions: "go to the house of Jesse" not "go to the house of Jesse, prepare an offering, and anoint the youngest David to be king." Samuel didn't have all the information, but he didn't need it. I definitely didn't have all the information (and I still don't), but I am still in my time of waiting. God is still sanctifying me. I honestly didn't know what that even meant. I had to look up the definition: to set apart for a sacred purpose. Even though I didn't know the purpose at the time, I was being set apart. If you are grieving, you may not know your purpose. Perhaps you were a caregiver, and since you lost your loved one, you don't know what your purpose is anymore. You may still be in your time of waiting. While you're waiting, continue to pray, read your Bible, and listen for God's one-step directions.

"Beyond our understanding, You are teaching us to trust." There are so many things I still don't understand. I don't understand why Travis had to die, or why Cole doesn't get to have his Daddy to grow up with. I don't know what my life will look like in five or ten years. Plenty of unknowns still remain in my life, but honestly, I'm okay with that (there's that peace that passes understanding). I am slowly learning what it means to trust God to take care of the things I don't understand. It feels a lot like letting go.

The bridge of the song says, "What the enemy meant for evil, You turn it for our good." I truly believe that is what happened for me, and can happen for anyone who has suffered devastating loss as well. The death of your loved one may break you, as my loss did me. But through the loss and grief, I have gained peace, strength, and hope I may have never otherwise obtained. I do believe we will be okay. It will take time, but we will be okay with God's help. I pray God will send you the peace and strength He has given me.

Reflections

1. Are there any songs you have already found comforting?

2. What type of music so you think would be most helpful to you?

3. How willing are you to listen to God's one-step instructions as Samuel did?

In the Silence

As powerful as music can be, and has been for me, I think the most powerful thing can simply be silence. Silence can be so difficult to obtain when a person's mind is racing with questions, fears, and uncertainty. Individuals who have suffered greatly get so focused on the pain everything else gets lost. We get so caught up in emotions we forget to just sit still for a second. It was months before I came to this realization.

Honestly, it was a song lyric that caught my attention (like I said, music can be a powerful thing). A song came on I had not heard in a long time called Praise You in This Storm.[5] I won't go over all the lyrics like I did before, but there were a few that stood out to me. The song opens with a sense of agony and despair, emotions you and I are familiar with. "I was sure by now, God You would have reached down and wiped my tears away... but once again, I say amen, and it's still raining." For months, all I could see or feel was the rain. I kept asking why when I really needed to be asking how? How was I going to move forward in life without Travis' hand to steady me? Others who have suffered loss might be asking how to move forward without your parent or the child you loved so dearly. The song gives the answer: "as the thunder rolls, I barely hear you whisper through the rain, I'm with you." When I finally stopped asking and started listening, that small voice reached down and reminded me I was not alone, no matter how isolated I felt. In the prayers of silence, I finally began to feel peace.

My heart was so desperately seeking shelter I had forgotten where the shelter was. All I needed was that little reminder, but I couldn't hear it. I do think God wanted to remind me for months, and He wants to remind you as well. But we have to stop shouting long enough to listen. Luckily for us, God is patient enough to wait for us to stop yelling. Like a steady parent, He stays present until we are able to calm down and listen.

Of course, one reminder wasn't enough for my human mind. I quickly fell back into my pain and stopped listening again. Occasionally, I would remember, but I couldn't overcome the pain long enough to listen again. Perhaps that is where you are. You know where to look for shelter, but you can't see through the storm to find it. The song, Praise You in This Storm describes this well: "I remember when I stumbled in the wind. You heard my cry and raised me up again." I kept calling out to God for help. I just wanted Him to somehow take away this pain. He did. It was brief moments of peace, but it was enough to sustain me. I may not have realized it at the time, but God was keeping my head just above the raging seas of my own thoughts and emotions. I may have felt as if I was drowning (and you might feel that way too), but God is there, holding our heads just above the waves. I often asked God, as the lyrics so eloquently say, "My strength is almost gone, how can I carry on if I can't find You?" Again, the question is "where are You?" By this point, I had been able to let go of the whys but still struggled with the where. I couldn't see how God was helping me in the months following Travis' death. I would feel the once calm waters start to rage again and ask, "Where are You, God?" I couldn't understand just because my own thoughts betrayed my heart with pain, it didn't mean that God had forgotten about me. It simply meant I had a grieving heart that needed help to recover. That's where God was. He was with me the entire time, but especially when the storm was raging the hardest. In chaos and darkness of the wind and rain, I had His small voice reminding me I wasn't alone. I simply needed to be still and listen.

When people feel they are beginning to drown, our instinct is to flail around for anything to pull ourselves up with. We yell for help. We desperately look up for anyone or anything to save us. This is where people fall into the trap of self-medication. The turn to alcohol to numb the feeling of panic and pain, but that will not save anyone. It took me a long time to learn it, and I am still learning, but the only way to be saved from drowning is to stop trying to save myself. Stop reaching out for something I could see. Stop looking around for something to hold on to. Nothing I could see or touch was enough to keep me afloat. Sure, it might work for a short while, but I would quickly start sinking again. I had to train my heart to reach for the unseen. Amid the panic, I had to learn how to relax, let go, and listen for the only One strong enough to keep me above the waters. I needed to remind myself (and maybe we all need to be reminded) of God's promise in Isaiah 43:2 "When you pass through the waters, I will be with you; and through the rivers, they shall not overwhelm you." If we can let go of our need to save ourselves, we can then allow God to save us from the raging seas. We simply need to learn to be still and listen for God to fulfill His promise; He will not allow the waters to overtake us.

Reflections

1. How have you handled your storm thus far? If you have been drowning, that's okay. There's no shame in struggling.

2. What have you been reaching for or calling out to in order to save yourself?

3. What comfort can you find in Isaiah 43:2? Have you felt God's help in your storm?

Perspectives: Melissa

What were the circumstances of your loss?

Early on in our third pregnancy, we were told that our baby was "incompatible with life" outside the womb. We were given the options to terminate the pregnancy or carry her to term, knowing she would not live more than a few moments or hours once she was born. Her diagnosis was acrania/anencephaly. We chose to celebrate her life for as long as we could, and we did. My two sons (ages four & six at the time) drew her pictures, felt her move, and loved her. Her heartbeat stopped on Good Friday in 2016. I gave birth to her still on Easter Sunday. She was our first daughter.

Can you describe your faith prior to the loss?

Both my husband and I grew up in Christian homes, have a relationship with Jesus, and participate in church as a family on a regular basis prior, during, and after our loss. I would describe my faith as pretty solid prior to our loss, but I had never really been through anything that tested my faith before. I remember the Sunday prior to us getting the news that we were singing "It Is Well" and I was praying to God that I couldn't really grasp the full meaning of the song because I hadn't really gone through anything really awful.

Can you describe your faith in the time after the loss?

My faith in the time after the loss was beyond my understanding. I spent a lot of time with God. The peace that came in the days immediately after our loss were surreal. I felt such a strong sense of His presence and Him walking me through the pain and those awful logistical issues of death: handing over her body to the funeral homes, writing her obituary, planning her memorial service, receiving her ashes in a box. It was all so hard, but there was no question of God's love and care through that time.

In what ways do you feel your faith was challenged due to loss?

It was the next several months that challenged my faith the most due to our loss. I became very angry at God. I couldn't sing worship songs about His faithfulness and goodness. I could just hear the word, "How could a good God do this to my baby?" I tried to fight the bitterness and allow the loss to make me better, like I heard people say, but in some ways I experienced both.

What do you wish you had known about grief?

I wish I had known how lonely grief would be. Initially we were surrounded by family and friends and felt a strong sense of community and support. And then people's lives went back to normal and I remember having to sit alone with my grief, and it was awful. I felt like no one really understood my unique grief, even if they had gone through something similar. I felt so alone.

What has helped or hindered your healing?

What has helped my healing is being honest and transparent with people when I can about my experience. Although my relationship with God is different now, I've learned to just embrace the reality that we are in – the good, the bad, and the ugly. My husband and I attended a grief retreat for child loss and I went to counseling. I read books and journaled. We received many mementos to celebrate her life and seeing those brought me peace and comfort. All of this contributed to our healing.

What hindered my healing was trying to act like I was healed sooner than I was. In public, I was trying to be brave, but at night when everyone was asleep, I wept deeply night after night. I became very angry and pushed my husband away many times – not intentionally, but I just didn't know how to be normal again. I guess I had to find a new normal I guess they say.

What is your greatest word of advice for those who are suffering grief and loss?

My advice to those who are suffering grief and loss is to be honest with yourself and those closest to you about how you're feeling. Find the people who you feel seem to be able to handle the ups and downs of grief without leaving or judging you. Be honest with God. He can handle the anger and He knows your circumstances and your heart fully. And be gracious with those who don't get it. Grief is socially awkward; our society does not know how to embrace it. I think we're learning, but people still say and do really awful things unintentionally of course and in the desire to help. You learn to give them a free pass, to choose to extend grace, and not allow the awkward words to sink in. Choose to focus on the truth you know and people who will remain when the dust settles.

The Long Haul

In my experience, the first months after a loss are all about survival. The goal of each day is just to make it through. It doesn't look pretty, and it sucks. Eventually, we learn how to survive each day. It may take someone two months, someone else five months, and another person over a year. No right or wrong timeline exists for this grief journey. The only one who can decide what one should or shouldn't be doing is the griever. After someone has made their way out of survival mode, he or she is in what I call the long haul. This is when the griever is relearning life without the person he or she lost. I had to relearn day-to-day life as a single mom. Others may have to readjust to not being in a hospital room or going to doctors' offices every day. Whatever the situation is, the individual recovering from loss is learning how to live his or her life in this new reality.

Honestly, this is where I needed God's help the most. I made it through survival mode with a lot of help from family and friends. I pray all who suffer great loss have a good support system to help you through survival. Not only in family or friends, but in a peer support group or counselor. In the long haul, though, the griever is responsible for rearranging his or her life and figuring out the new normal. It is a confusing and frustrating time. Some days are great, and a person will feel like he or she is doing really well. The next day, that same person could be a mess and feel like he or she is starting over again. Please know this is normal. Grief is not a straight path; someone grieving will go forward, go backward, take the unexpected turns, and get knocked off the path. Most of all, the long haul is just that: a long journey of a lot of work.

It is easy to think God failed me when He allowed Travis to die. I would expect people to feel as if God failed them when He allowed their spouse, child, parent, or friend to die. I don't believe He did. I don't know why we must go through this loss, but that's not for us to understand. What I do know is through the loss, God has been more apparent to me than He had ever been before. It's not that He wasn't there before; I was just more willing to look for Him because I had lost the most important person in my life. I didn't have Travis to lean on anymore. I was falling hard and had no one to fall on. Yes, I had people who were amazing to support me, but family and friends can only do so much. I honestly believe even Travis wouldn't have been able to hold me up this time. I was falling too far and too hard. The only one strong enough to help was God, and He did. I had hit rock bottom and shattered into a million pieces. I didn't even know how to start picking up the pieces, let alone put myself together. One of my favorite worship songs, Francesca Battistelli's "Defender,"[6] says, "You picked up all my pieces, put me back together. You are the defender of my heart." I had to allow God to enter into my pain, but He picked up all the pieces of my shattered heart. He didn't do it for me, but He helped me begin to heal.

Another song I love, called "Do It Again,"[7] talks about doing the work. The verse says, "Walking around these walls, I thought by now they'd fall." That is a reference to the Biblical story of Jericho, which some readers might be familiar with. Joshua 6 gives the account of the Israelites' encounter with the stronghold city of Jericho. It was impenetrable. There was no conceivable way for Joshua and the Israelite army to take the city until Joshua heard from God. Joshua was told to march around the walls once a day for six days. Just march, nothing else. No war cries, no attacks on the city. Simply march around the city with the Ark of the Covenant.

On the seventh day, the army was to march around the city seven times. On the seventh time, the trumpets were sounded, and the army let out a large shout. The walls of Jericho fell. The song speaks to the tiring task of marching around the walls. Below is a simulated image depicting what the walls of Jericho would look like based on archeological finds.[8]

According to archeological finds,[8] Jericho was a total of nine-to-ten acres in area. That is equivalent to about twelve football fields. Imagine lining up twelve football fields and marching around it. Add to that the ominous walls. The walls were built as a two-layer defense into the bedrock. The base of the

103

first wall was a stone retaining wall estimated to be about thirteen feet high. The retaining wall had a mudbrick wall atop it, which was around twenty-three feet in height. Farther up the embankment, there was another mudbrick wall, similar to the lower one. It is estimated the base of the upper wall was forty-six feet above ground level. Both mudbrick walls were about six feet thick. From ground level to the top of the upper wall was almost seventy feet. That is close to a seven-story building! Have you ever stood at the base of a seven-story building? I imagine it would seem impossible to overcome, but God knew otherwise. It was likely a long seven days, and I'm sure even the most faithful soldiers began to question the wisdom of God's direction. The work of those days was necessary to reach the result of victory.

The walls built around our grief may seem just as impenetrable to us. How could I possibly overcome such sorrow and pain? For so long, I felt as though I was making no progress, even though I was doing everything I could for myself and relying on God for the rest. I can't remember how many times I asked myself and God, how long do I have to do this? How long will this suffering last? I wanted my walls to fall so much sooner than they did. But if they had, I would not have the faith and peace I have now. Just like the Israelites, I had to depend on God to break down my barriers. But I also had to put in the work in the meantime, just as the Israelites had to walk around the walls.

When someone is in the long haul of walking around the impenetrable grief, it seems pointless. It is a long and tiring process. If you are grieving and haven't reached the long haul yet, don't be discouraged. It is tiring, but necessary. If you are in the long haul now, don't lose hope. Keep walking and trust God will help with the rest. God will bring down those walls when you least expect it.

Reflections

1. Do you feel you have reached the long haul? Or are you still in survival mode?

2. If you are in the long haul, how do you relate to the Israelites around Jericho?

3. If you have already reached your victory, what did you do to get there? How can you move forward from here?

The Holiday Struggle

In survival mode, one may or may not even participate in holidays, and that's okay. Once someone reaches the long haul, he or she has to figure out what to do for the holidays. Each person has their top holidays that are the hardest for them. For me, it is Father's Day and Christmas. Since I have already explained my Father's Day solution earlier, I will focus this chapter on Christmas. Whatever holiday may be difficult, please keep reading. Even though I will be using Christmas, the concept can apply to any holiday someone may struggle with.

Christmas is particularly difficult because both Travis and I loved Christmas. Travis also passed away just a few weeks before Cole's first Christmas. I wanted absolutely nothing to do with Christmas that year. I forced myself to do it, but only because it was Cole's first Christmas. By the next year, I had reached the long haul. I had to choose what I was going to do. Holidays are odd during grief. They are such a blaring reminder of what has been lost. With every laugh or gift, everyone in the room can be instantly reminded of the one who should be there but isn't. Traditions change, plans are altered. That empty chair or un-bought gift is just another sign of what, or more accurately, who is missing. With seemingly constant reminders of loss, we can easily forget to see what *is* there. If we are not careful, we will so easily allow this grief and sorrow to steal our joy. If we aren't watchful of our own mind and spirit, we can fall into the trap of missing Christmas. Not that we won't be in the room, but we may not be participants. Instead of being the shepherds or the Magi, we become King Herod. Herod knew of Jesus' birth; he was aware of the first Christmas. Instead of celebrating it, he cowered from it. Matthew 2:3 says, "When King Herod heard this, he was disturbed..." The 'this' in the verse is referring to Jesus' birth as King of the Jews. As the ruling king, Herod felt threatened by this newly born King. He believed his position was potentially no longer safe or secure. We can easily fall into this trap when grieving. While Herod believed he was threatened by a new life, we can sometimes feel threatened by our loss. While we might not fear losing a political role, we do fear the loss or change of many other roles. We come to believe that in our loss, we are no longer safe or secure. Yes, grief and loss will knock us off our feet and make our lives unsteady for a while. It doesn't mean it has to stay that way.

In my situation, I had to decide what I would do for Christmas, as well as all the other holidays and special occasions. Because I have a toddler, it was easier for me to choose to stay involved and keep it a special day. Some traditions have changed. I see my in-laws on a different day instead of splitting Christmas Day between the two families. Other traditions haven't changed. Travis and I always went to a Christmas store to get a special ornament for that year. I still went. I cried in the middle of the store, but I went. I will continue to go each year. It is bittersweet without Travis there, but it is fun to watch Cole get excited about the lights and seeing Santa.

There are some 'special' days I choose not to participate in. This year, we went to a golfing place on what would have been Travis' 30th birthday. He had asked to go there for his birthday, so we went. It was hard, but it was still fun. I do not know yet what I will do for his birthday in the future if anything. Some make a "memorial day" from the day their loved one passed. I choose not to. It will always be a sad day for me, but I do not want Cole to know what day it is. It can be sad for me; it doesn't need to be a sad day for him. Whatever our hard days are, we get to choose what to do. Some people may try to make us do something we don't want to. Please don't let them force a griever to do something he or she is not comfortable with. Word of advice on a practical thing for my grieving readers: If you go anywhere, always drive yourself. Wherever you go, whether it be a holiday party or wedding, always give yourself a way out if you need it. Ultimately, we get to decide what to do or not do. If we go somewhere and want to leave, it is perfectly fine to leave. Only we can decide what is right for us and our grief.

Reflections

1. My hardest holidays are Christmas and Father's Day. Which days will be your hardest?

2. Have you already created some new traditions or plans for the hard holidays?

3. Do you feel like you will be able to step away or cry if you need to? If not, is there a support person you can bring with you to help?

Perspectives: Beth

What were the circumstances of your loss?

My husband fell from the attic and hit his head on a concrete step. He was unconscious. He had emergency surgery and it didn't help. He never regained consciousness. We took him off life-support after five days and he passed away two minutes later.

Can you describe your faith prior to your loss?

I have known the Lord my whole life. My faith in the Lord was very strong before my husband's accident.

Can you describe your faith in the time after the loss?

My faith is still very strong because I know the Lord is in control and He loves and cares for me.

In what ways did you feel your faith was challenged due to loss?

I prayed for God to heal Dwight according to His Will, whether He healed him miraculously (despite what the doctors were saying), he healed him partially (to be able to come home with me, but may have been in a wheelchair) or to give him ultimate healing and take him home to Heaven. I have a picture of Dwight, my Mom and I, and I said to the Lord during Dwight's stay in the hospital, "I do not want to be the only one alive in this picture." It was where I was at mentally and emotionally that day. In my heart, I knew Dwight was going to go to Heaven and I asked the Lord, "Why are you taking away the two people I love the most (my Mom and Dwight) away from me ten months apart?" I asked Him to show me His purpose in this. I am choosing to grow through this and to become better and not bitter.

What do you wish you had known about grief?

Grief can hit you out of nowhere, when you least expect it.

What has helped or hindered your healing?

The Lord has helped me tremendously. My family and friends have been praying, listening and have been and continue to be here for me.

What is your greatest word of advice for those who are suffering grief and loss?

My advice would be to hold on to Jesus and never let go of Him. Cry out, pray, scream and yell at the top of your lungs if you need to. Allow others to help you, even if you are fiercely independent. Talk with your family and friends about what you are feeling. Share with them where you are at emotionally, mentally, physically and spiritually. Ask the Lord to hold you close and help you to heal your hurting heart.

The Ultimate Choice

"We must be willing to let go of the life we've planned so as to have the life that's waiting for us."

–Joseph Campbell[9]

I heard this quote at the end of a TV show I was watching, and it got me thinking a bit. At first, I was almost appalled at the suggestion I had to "let go" of my life with Travis to live the rest of my life is in front of me. So often in grief, we see moving forward in life without our loved one as moving on or letting go of our previous life we had with them. I see it a bit differently. I see it as a delicate balance you have to find within your own life. I cannot live my life as if Travis were still alive. That is neither healthy nor sustainable. However, it is equally as unhealthy to live my life as if he was never a part of it. There has to be a balance. We have to figure out how to continue living our day-to-day lives without our loved one physically with us. My life did not end when Travis died, nor did it start. It simply changed. Well, not simply. Quite complexly changed actually, but changed nevertheless. To "let go" of Travis would be equivalent to erasing him from my heart and memory. I cannot, nor would I be willing to do that. What I needed to do, and I believe I have done is to let go of the life I expected to have with him. I had to find a way to be okay on my own, and I hope I have helped others do the same. We will never be without our loved one completely. Travis will always be a part of my life, just as my childhood or teenage years are. Unlike those years, I cannot reduce him to a phase or stage of my life. He was much more than that, and I am sure any lost loved one would be. Having Travis in my life, and losing him, made me who I am. I am a very different person today than I was the day before he died. His death forced me to find a way to survive, even if I didn't want to. In the process of surviving, I had to learn and accept what life was going to be. His loss was not something I could change; I had no control over death. What I can control is what I do in the time following his death. We have that control.

It is said time heals all things, but I disagree. I think it is what we do in the time that will or will not lead to healing. Surviving grief and thriving from it takes a lot of work. I had help; I needed it. I depended on God for strength and peace, and a core group of people for everything else. At first, I couldn't even care for myself, let alone my baby. But as time went on, I slowly pushed myself back up and fought through it. Don't get me wrong; I stumbled many times. There were so many moments I thought I couldn't do it anymore. I couldn't have done it on my own. Only by holding on to the peace God had given me was I able to muster enough energy to carry on. Fast forward to today. Today, I have my new normal as a single mom. My life is very different than I expected it to be, but I am okay with that. I have learned to release my grip, not from my love for Travis, but from daily life I had with him. It is through this I am able to enjoy the life I have now. It is not an easy thing to do; it takes time and a lot of effort to learn the balance. But it is essential to continuing to live and enjoy life. I can, and will always hold on to the love I have for Travis, but I can also embrace the new normal that exists in his physical absence.

What we need to realize, and try to focus on if we can, is our loss is another piece to the puzzle of our lives. The pieces add to the puzzle and make it the beautiful picture it is. This piece definitely is not our favorite, but it doesn't have to ruin the puzzle. My sister was once putting together a puzzle to frame in her firstborn's nursery. It was a beautiful scene from the original Winnie the Pooh. While she was working on the puzzle, one of the pieces fell to the floor. Her little Pomeranian, Bear, got ahold of it and chewed it up a bit. The piece was permanently damaged. To some, that would have ruined the entire puzzle. She would not allow it. She still used the piece to complete the beautiful scene. You can still see the damaged piece right in the center of the scene.

Honestly, I think we have a lot to learn from this damaged puzzle piece. My sister was putting together something very special, a gift for her first baby. This puzzle is like our own lives. We put it together so carefully to make sure every piece is placed where we think it needs to be. But just like in life, one of the pieces falls. For all who grieve a loss, the fallen piece is the death of our loved one. The first loss was the death itself. Anyone who works hard on a puzzle they care about will be panicked when a piece gets dropped. They will drop what they are doing and frantically search for it. To add to the upsetting moment of the lost puzzle piece, the dog started to chew it up. Isn't that a pretty good analogy for our puzzles when grief hits? We first have to deal with the shock and emotion coming from the loss itself. Once we find the piece, we hope to find it intact, but circumstances of loss chew up that piece of our hearts and lives just as Bear chewed up the dropped puzzle piece. That beautiful gift which was so special to my sister was seemingly destroyed, especially since that piece fit right in the middle of the image. The image of our lives is damaged by the loss of someone so important to us. The damaged piece of losing a loved one will definitely alter the center of our life's image. But just because it is altered doesn't mean it is ruined. The beauty still remains in the damage. My sister still used the piece to complete the puzzle, and it is still hanging on the wall all these years later. She once said Bear just wanted to be a part of the process. While losing Travis was devastating and damaging, to say the least, it is still a piece of my life's puzzle. I cannot remove the piece completely, or the image will be incomplete. My life would be missing a large piece if I tried to remove the hurt of losing him. To remove pain, I would have to remove Travis. I would gladly accept the damage and pain to make sure Travis' piece in my puzzle remains.

Everyone who is grieving has a decision to make, and that decision will need to be made many times. It might be once a day or 100 times a day, but it has to be a conscious decision. We have to decide whether we will find joy in the altered image or let the damage destroy the beauty. Will the change enhance the beauty? Or will the change be allowed to destroy the image? I pray the grievers will find God's peace and hold tightly to it, not only in grief but always.

This is not the end of the conversation. I hope those who are grieving will find a support system that can help them through this pain. No one should do this alone. I pray those who are trying to be a part of that system have learned what they can do to be as supportive as possible in someone else's healing. For those who have more questions, visit www.faithingrief.com. There, questions and comments can be posted.

Reflections

1. What does your puzzle piece look like? Where does it fit in your image?

2. What can you do to embrace your damaged piece and let it be a part of your beauty?

3. If bitterness has taken ahold of your heart, can you identify ways to help yourself release that anger?

Appendix A

These are the songs that have been helpful to me in my time of grief.

I Won't Let You Go – Switchfoot

You're Gonna Be Okay – Jenn Johnson

Joy Invicible – Switchfoot

Sovereign Over Us – Shane & Shane

Thrive – Switchfoot

Defender – Francesca Battistelli

Against the Voices – Switchfoot

All I Need – Switchfoot

Do It Again – Shane & Shane

The Day That I Found God – Switchfoot

Hope Is The Anthem – Switchfoot

Praise You In This Storm – Casting Crowns

Live It Well – Switchfoot

Only Hope – Switchfoot

Way Maker - Sinach

Restless – Switchfoot

It Is Well – Bethel Music

The Strength To Let Go – Switchfoot

Take My Fire – Switchfoot

Voices – Switchfoot

Even If - MercyMe

We're Gonna Be Alright – Switchfoot

Where I Belong – Switchfoot

I Am Not Alone – Kari Jobe

Where The Light Shines Through - Switchfoot

References

[1] Quotes, (n.d). Retrieved from https://www.mygriefassist.com.au/inspiration-resources/quotes/

[2] Moore, B. (2010). *David: Seeking a heart like his.* Lifeway Christian Resources.

[3] Bethel Music (feat. Kristene DiMarco). (2014). It Is Well [Song]. On *You Make Me Brave.* Bethel Music.

[4] Shane & Shane. (2016). Sovereign Over Us [Song]. On *Worship Initiative, Vol. 11.* Wellhouse Records.

[5] Casting Crowns. (2005). Praise You In This Storm [Song]. On *Lifesong.* Reunion Records.

[6] Francesca Battistelli. (2019). Defender [Song]. On *Defender (Single Version).* Word Entertainment LLC.

[7]Shane & Shane. (2018). Do It Again [Song]. On *Worship Initiative, Vol. 16.* Wellhouse Records.

[8]Wood, B. (1999). The Walls of Jericho. Retrieved from https://answersingenesis.org/archaeology/the-walls-of-jericho/

[9]BrainyQuote. (n.d.). Retrieved from https://www.brainyquote.com/quotes/joseph_campbell_386014?img=2